FACT FINDERS

Educational adviser: Arthur Razzell

Rockets and Space Travel

Kenneth Gatland, F.R.A.S., F.B.I.S.

Illustrated by Terry Collins, F.S.I.A.,
Eric Jewell Associates and Barry Salter
Designed by Faulkner/Marks Partnership

Macmillan Education Limited

1976 Macmillan Education Limited
First printed 1976, reprinted 1978

Published in the United
States by Silver Burdett
Company, Morristown, N.J.
1978 Printing

ISBN 0-382-06243-4

Library of Congress
Catalog Card No. 78-64661

Rockets and Space Travel

Rockets through the Ages   page 4

Rockets and Satellites   page 6

What Satellites Do   page 8

Moon Probes   page 10

Man in Space   page 12

Man on the Moon   page 14

Homes in Space   page 16

Exploring the Planets   page 18

The Future   page 20

Glossary   page 22

Index   page 23

Rockets through the Ages

The Chinese used fire-arrows in warfare nearly one thousand years ago. In 1804 Sir William Congreve invented iron-cased war rockets (below) filled with gunpowder.

Fifty years later, the first line-carrying rockets were made to rescue shipwrecked sailors.

Chinese fire-arrows

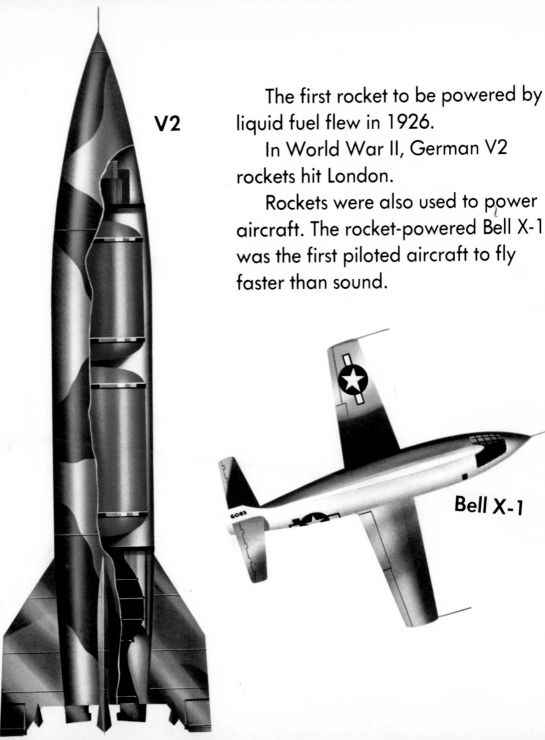

V2

The first rocket to be powered by liquid fuel flew in 1926.

In World War II, German V2 rockets hit London.

Rockets were also used to power aircraft. The rocket-powered Bell X-1 was the first piloted aircraft to fly faster than sound.

Bell X-1

Rockets and Satellites

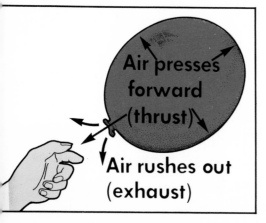

Air presses forward (thrust)

Air rushes out (exhaust)

To understand how a rocket works, blow up a balloon, and let it go. The balloon shoots forward as air rushes out (left). A rocket works in the same kind of way. It is propelled by the forward pressure (thrust) of its exhaust gases. Below are the two main kinds of rocket.

LIQUID FUEL ROCKET

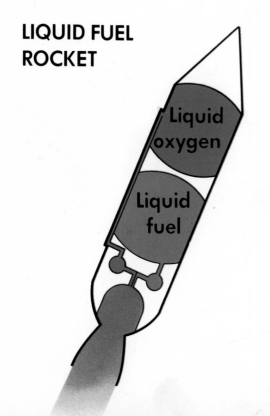

Liquid oxygen

Liquid fuel

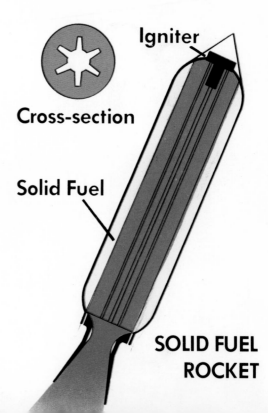

Igniter

Cross-section

Solid Fuel

SOLID FUEL ROCKET

Satellites are small, man-made 'moons' that circle the Earth. They are launched by high-speed rockets with several sections, or stages. The satellite shown below was launched in 1974 by a multi-stage rocket called a Titan 3C. This used both liquid and solid fuels.

How satellite opens in space

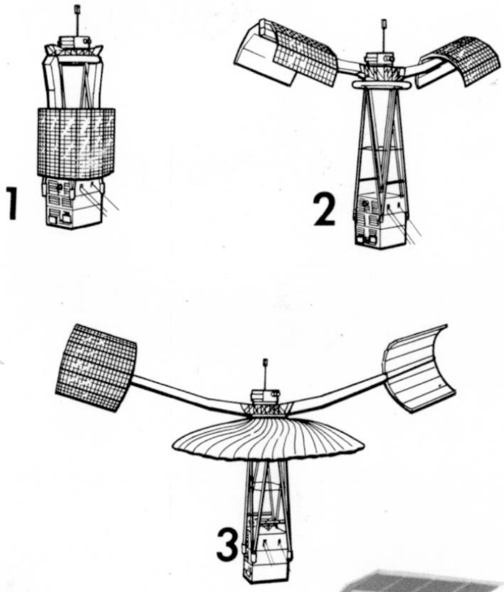

1

2

3

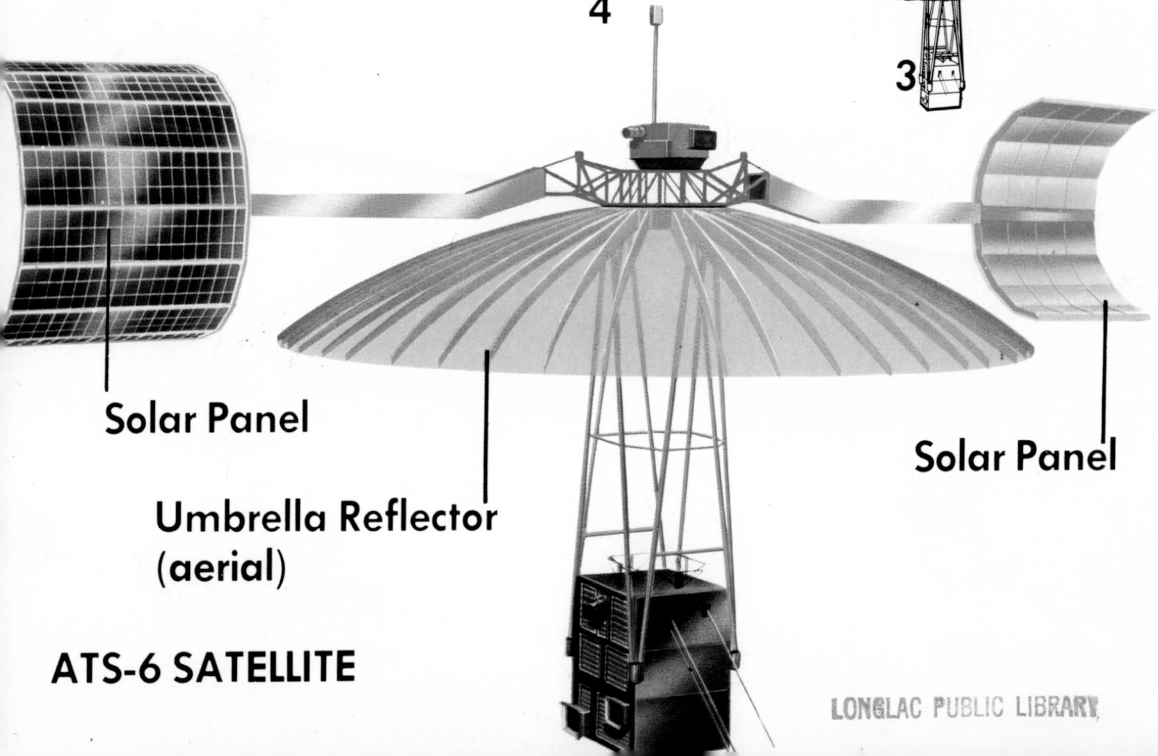

4

Solar Panel

Umbrella Reflector (aerial)

Solar Panel

ATS-6 SATELLITE

What Satellites Do

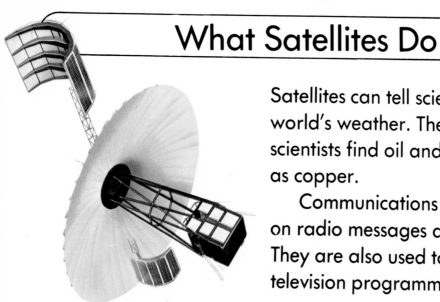

Satellites can tell scientists about the world's weather. They can also help scientists find oil and minerals, such as copper.

Communications satellites pass on radio messages and signals. They are also used to pass on television programmes.

ATS-6 satellite

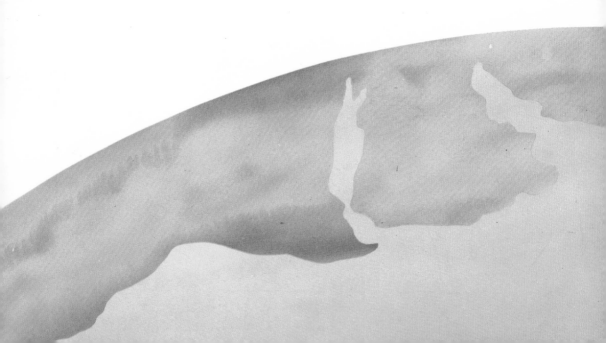

Satellites help in teaching. For example, one satellite can send television programmes to thousands of towns and villages in India.

The Earth takes 24 hours to spin right round. Communications satellites normally take the same time to circle the Earth.

Television in a village in India

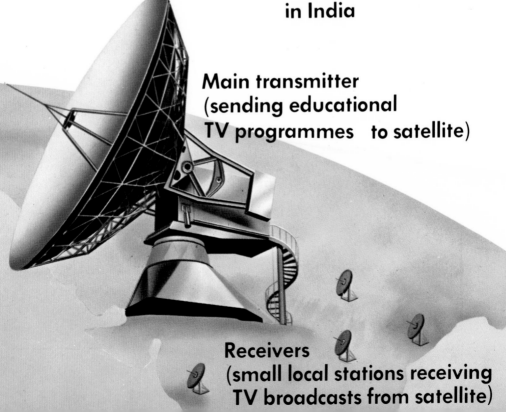

Main transmitter (sending educational TV programmes to satellite)

Receivers (small local stations receiving TV broadcasts from satellite)

Moon Probes

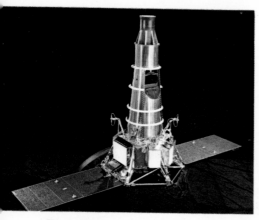

Ranger 7

Before men landed on the Moon, probes were sent to get information. U.S. Ranger spacecraft (left) sent T.V. pictures before crash-landing. Then, Lunar Orbiters (Moon circlers) flew round the Moon taking more photographs. Probes called Surveyors landed on the Moon to test the soil.

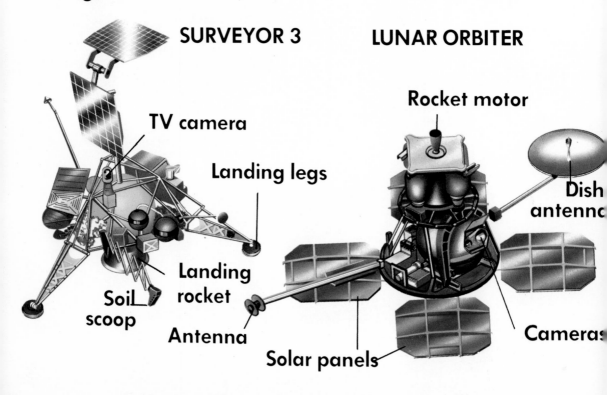

SURVEYOR 3

TV camera

Landing legs

Landing rocket

Soil scoop

Antenna

LUNAR ORBITER

Rocket motor

Dish antenna

Solar panels

Cameras

Russian scientists made probes to bring back pieces of Moon rock. Luna 16 (right) was the first probe which brought back samples of the Moon's soil.

Lunokhod (below) is a Russian Moon car without a driver. It was steered by radio signals from Earth.

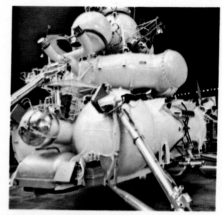

Luna 16

Lunokhod

Man in Space

The first man in space was the Russian Yuri Gagarin, in 1961. The following year, John Glenn became the first U.S. astronaut to orbit the Earth.

Tests by manned spacecraft prepared the way for landing on the Moon. Space walks helped solve problems of weightlessness in space.

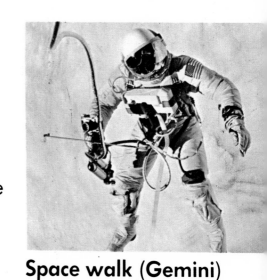

Space walk (Gemini)

GEMINI

Equipment module

Landing parachutes

Descent module

Retro-rockets

Solar panels

SOYUZ

Orbital module

Docking antenna

Equipment module

Oxygen pack
system

Helmet

ASTRONAUT

Visor

Control box

Sun glass pocket

Lifeline
(carrying
oxygen
supply)

Glove

Lunar overshoe

**Apollo
Lunar module**

Men first landed on the Moon on 20 July 1969. They were U.S. astronauts Neil Armstrong and Edwin Aldrin. They set out instruments, and obtained 21.8 kilogrammes of Moon soil and rocks.

By the end of 1972, 12 men had walked on the Moon in six different places. Lunar Rovers were used on the last three visits.

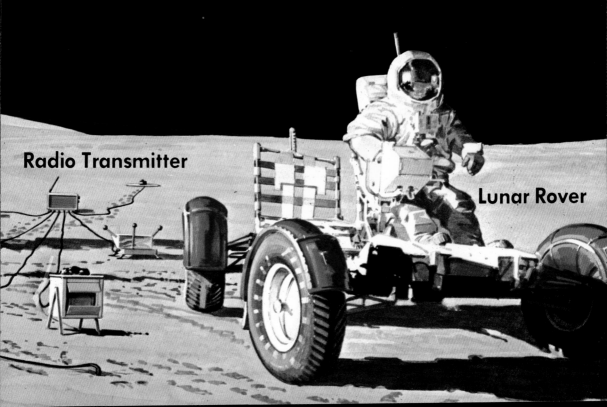

Radio Transmitter

Lunar Rover

The next big advance was the U.S. Skylab. This was damaged during its launching in 1973. However, three different three-man teams visited and repaired it. It was used as a base for about 170 days while astronauts carried out experiments.

To prepare for space stations, the U.S. and U.S.S.R. combined their experience to test a link-up of spacecraft in space in 1975.

Skylab crew launch

Link-up between Apollo and Soyuz

Apollo (U.S.)

Soyuz (U.S.S.R.

KYLAB

**Apollo
Command and
Service modules**

Docking ports

**Airlock (for entry
and exit)**

Solar wing

**Sleeping
Compartment**

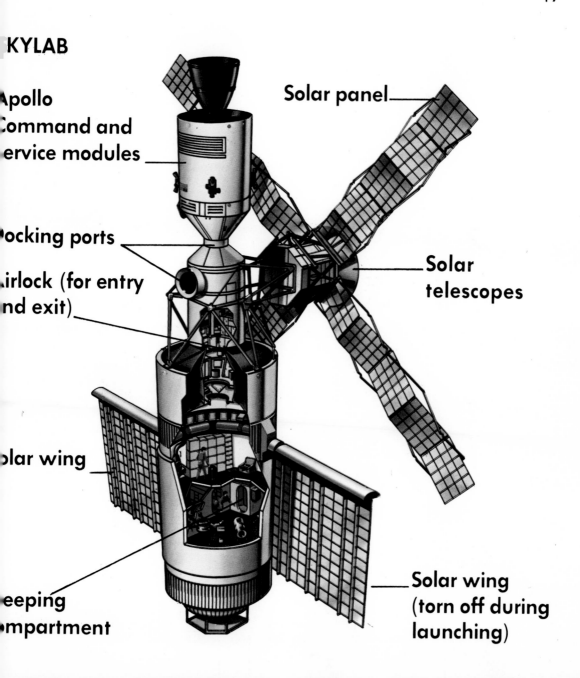

Solar panel

**Solar
telescopes**

**Solar wing
(torn off during
launching)**

Exploring the Planets

Unmanned space probes have sent back T.V. pictures of the planets Venus, Mercury, Mars, and Jupiter.

Russian instruments penetrated the swirling clouds of Venus.

U.S. Mariner probes took detailed pictures of the surface of Mars (right). Viking Landers were sent to probe for life on Mars.

The surface of Mars

Mercury Venus Earth Mars   **Jupiter**

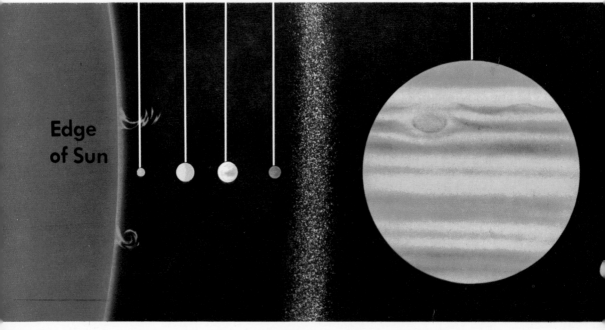

Edge of Sun

Viking Orbiter

Viking Lander

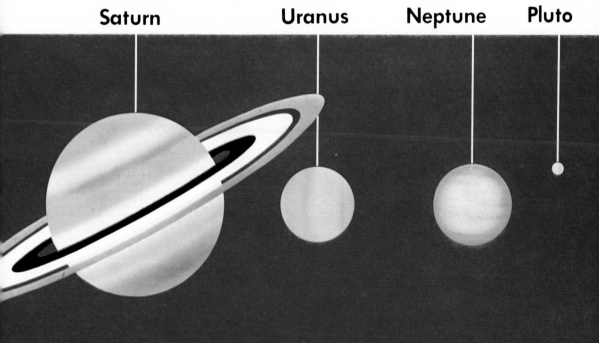

Saturn

Uranus

Neptune

Pluto

The Future

In the 1980's the re-usable Space Shuttle will be introduced, greatly reducing the cost of space travel.

The winged 'orbiter' will take off in the same way as a rocket. It will fly satellites and people into orbit and then return to base.

A big space station could be built from parts carried up piece by piece.

2. Boosters away (to be re-used)

1. Launch

Cutaway showing pressurised European 'Space Lab'

Glossary

Astronaut   A person who travels into space.

Exhaust Gases   Used-up fuel released from a motor in the form of gases.

Experiments   Tests to find out or prove whether an idea is correct or not.

Fire-arrow   An arrow with burning materials attached to the shaft.

Gunpowder   An explosive powder used in early rockets. Today, it is used in fireworks.

Link-up   The connecting of two separate spacecraft.

Multi-Stage Rocket   A rocket made up of two or more parts, or stages. Each stage is thrown off after its fuel has been burnt.

Orbit   A regular path taken by a body or object circling another in space. The Earth takes a year to complete its orbit around the Sun.

Planet   A body which orbits a star. In the Solar System, the planets orbit the Sun, which is a star.

Probes   Instruments sent to explore space. They carry no astronauts, but they can send back information to Earth.

Propelled   Driven or pushed forward.

Weightlessness   The floating of people or objects in space.

Index

Aircraft   5
Aldrin, E.   15
Astronauts   12, 15, 16
Armstrong, N.   15
Bell X-1   5
Earth   7, 9, 11, 12
Fire-arrows   4
Gagarin, Y.   12
Glenn, J.   12
Gunpowder   4
Jupiter   18
Liquid fuel   5, 7
Luna 16   11
Lunar Orbiters   10
Lunar Rovers   15
Lunokhod   11
Mariner   18
Mars   18
Mercury   18
Minerals   8
Moon   10, 11, 12, 15
Moon soil   10, 11, 15
Multi-stage rocket   7

Oil   8
Orbiter   20
Photographs 10, 18
Probes   10, 11, 18
Ranger   10
Satellites   7, 8, 9
Signals   8, 11
Skylab   16
Solid fuel   7
Space   12, 16, 20
Spacecraft   10, 12, 16
Space shuttle   20
Space stations   16, 20
Space walks   12
Surveyor   10
Television programmes   8, 9
Titan 3C   7
V2 rocket   5
Venus   18
Viking   18
Warfare   4
Weightlessness   12
World War II   5

2 3 4 5 6 7 8 9 10—· R —85 84 83 82 81 80